IMAGES
of America

UPPER
ST. JOHN VALLEY

Aerial view of the winding St. John River, with roads on both sides of the river—one road in Maine, the other in New Brunswick, Canada.

IMAGES
of America

UPPER
ST. JOHN VALLEY

Frank H. Sleeper
with the Madawaska Historical Society and Others

ARCADIA
PUBLISHING

Published by Arcadia Publishing
Charleston SC, Chicago IL, Portsmouth NH, San Francisco CA

Library of Congress Catalog Card Number: 2007921773

For all general information contact Arcadia Publishing at:
Telephone 843-853-2070
Fax 843-853-0044
E-mail sales@arcadiapublishing.com
For customer service and orders:
Toll-Free 1-888-313-2665

Visit us on the Internet at www.arcadiapublishing.com

Simeon Martin plowing his field *au grand ruisseau* in the backsettlements of St. David (a section of Madawaska) in the early 1920s.

Contents

Reverend Leonide Nicknair, a Franciscan, celebrating his first mass at St. Mary's Church, Eagle Lake, in 1952. The Nicknairs from the Valley were priests, nuns, and nurses who engaged in a variety of humanitarian callings all over Maine in the mid-twentieth century.

Introduction

The concept of "Two Maines" as popularized and possibly invented by Dick Barringer years ago is probably more valid today than ever. But within those two regions, there are varied sub-regions, and at another level, many separate communities of Maine. Take the far north of Aroostook County, for example. Ethnically, as you travel north in Aroostook, you move gradually from English-Irish stock with a small Franco-American minority and a block of Native Americans to predominantly Franco-American folk in the Upper St. John Valley with only a Scotch-Irish-English minority in the town of Allagash at the northwest end of the organized Valley population. In the midst of the gradual shift of the area to Franco-Americans are the Swedish-based towns of New Sweden, Stockholm, and Westmanland.

Somewhere not too far north of these Swedish towns, Aroostook County becomes overwhelmingly Franco-American. One must always remember that the international boundary between the United States and Canada in this area wasn't settled until the Webster-Ashburton Treaty of 1842. Much of that boundary settlement ran along the upper St. John River. It seems doubtful that the Acadians and the Quebecois on the U.S. side of the new line were unhappy with the land split. Both had long histories of poor treatment from the English. The Acadians of the valley, of course, had been dispossessed twice by the English: in 1755, with the great dispersal of Acadians all along the East Coast as far as Louisiana from their Nova Scotia homes; and after the Revolutionary War, when their new homes in New Brunswick and Nova Scotia were given to Loyalists expelled from the United States.

Both the Acadians and the Quebecois were French-speaking and both were inheritors of French customs and traditions. A person can show photographs of those customs and traditions as exemplified in the Upper St. John Valley, but one cannot show photographs of the spirit of the people living there. It is a spirit of independence, of hard work, of survival. The Acadians came first in any real numbers to Madawaska; the Quebecois, through the voyageurs and others, may have come even sooner, but they arrived in the New World as trappers and traders, not as settlers. Because they have such a unique history and were an early example of one form of ethnic cleansing, the Acadians have received more publicity than the Quebecois, who overflowed from that province all over northern New England. Acadian and Quebecois names can still be traced in the Upper St. John Valley, but the two French-speaking groups have now become intricately mixed by intermarriage.

This bilingual population has always been one of Maine's great resources, though for long years the state government didn't appreciate that fact. However, if the province of Quebec ever does become independent, the value of that resource will become much more obvious. Trade deals must be made. The roads to Estcourt Station on the border and to St. Pamphile in Quebec must be taken over by the State and upgraded into excellent year-round roads. There may even come a day when Quebec will wish to join the United States. That could be spurred on by the American residents of the Upper St. John Valley.

But this is far in the future, if ever. For now, we have the Franco-Americans of the Valley, staunchly Democrat in their politics—a carry-over partly from the help they received under Franklin Roosevelt's New Deal. Yet, they must be considered conservative Democrats, with their strong beliefs in family, religion, and, until quite recently, farming. Many of them may be closer to "Clinton-type" Democrats.

The emphasis on family is part of what makes up the greatest strength of Maine. Family reunions are a constant of Upper St. John Valley life. Interest in genealogy seems to be everywhere. There is great respect for ancestors and there is great respect for the history of each Valley community. For example, former Maine Supreme Court Justice Elmer Violette moved some years ago to his present home on Violette Street near Violette Brook in the town of Van Buren. That town was called Violette before its name was changed to honor Martin Van Buren. Violettes were among the first settlers and have been prominent in the community and in state politics from the very beginning. Justice Violette moved from a smaller home on Main Street that had been in his family for generations. His present home is on land owned by Violettes in the past.

Here, respect for family and traditional values is joined with respect for religion and its traditional values. However, there is more to it than just that. You will notice I have put some priests in the chapter Doers and Shakers; that is because priests in the Valley have been known for the improvements they have started in their communities. They have not sat back and done nothing just because there has never been a Franco-American Roman Catholic bishop of the diocese of Portland, in spite of the fact that a vast majority of Catholics in Maine are of that ethnic persuasion. These priests have concentrated on improving their own parishes, and have had a tremendous impact on the communities of the Valley as a result.

A third stabilizing factor until recent years was the focus on agriculture in the area. Since World War II, the number of farms has decreased dramatically. What has survived are large, heavily mechanized farms. Many citizens work for Fraser Paper's mills in Madawaska and across the St. John River in Edmundston, New Brunswick. Some have set up their own businesses; no longer are Valley businesses run and owned by outsiders. The Upper St. John Valley is a part of the United States unlike any other. Here are a few views of it.

Frank H. Sleeper

One

The River

A ferryboat that went across the St. John River from Fort Kent to Clair, New Brunswick, c. 1900. Major William Dickey wanted international bridges built in Fort Kent, Madawaska, and Van Buren, but he did not live to see that goal accomplished.

A ferryboat crossing between Madawaska and Edmundston, New Brunswick, in 1919. Solomon Beaulieu (left) and Eugene Bouchard are in this photograph with two unidentified women.

International bridge between Madawaska and Edmundston in the process of construction in 1921. Major Dickey's dreams were finally coming true.

The completed international bridge between Edmundston and Madawaska overlooking the New Brunswick community. The building to the right is the Edmundston courthouse and jail.

The St. John River in 1928, the international boundary between Madawaska and Edmundston. This was after the Fraser Paper mill was built in Madawaska. Later, pipelines carried material from the other mill in Edmundston and vice versa across the river.

The dam on Long Lake, Allagash River, as it was being built in 1919. The dam routed water until it was washed out in the 1950s. St. Agatha in the Valley is on another Long Lake, south of the St. John River.

Men inside a log drive boom sorting out logs in the St. John River at Van Buren, c. 1910.

Two

Family

Golden wedding of Dr. and Mrs. Thomas Pelletier in Van Buren, July 12, 1919. The couple are second and third from the left in the front row. From left to right are as follows: (front row) Leola Pelletier, Mrs. Thomas Pelletier, Dr. Thomas Pelletier, and Reverend Louis Pelletier; (back row) Dr. Ludget Pelletier, Mrs. L.P. (Alma) Thibodeau, Joseph Pelletier, Mrs. W. (Rosalie) Daicole, Alphonse Pelletier, and Helene Pelletier.

Golden wedding anniversary of Mr. and Mrs. Pierre A. Cyr, January 10, 1949, at Lille, one of the towns between Van Buren and Madawaska on the St. John. From left to right are as follows: (front row) Msgr. Armand E. Cyr, Sister Aline, Mrs. Cyr, Mr. Cyr, and Sister Armand (Gertrude); (back row) Dr. Donat P. Cyr, Simone Cyr, J. Wilfred Cyr, Rose Cyr Levesque (wife of Dr. Romeo Levesque), Mrs. (Alice) Lawrence Violette, Edward P. Cyr, Mrs. (Josephine) Albert Cyr, and Patrick Cyr.

Golden wedding anniversary of Mr. and Mrs. Alex Levesque in 1956 in Madawaska. From left to right are as follows: (first row) Alphie, Mr. Levesque, Mrs. (Blanche) Arthur Pelletier, Arthie, Dorine Levesque, and Mrs. (Azelie) Philip LaCroix; (back row) Eddie Dionne, Bertha Levesque (Mrs. Alphie), Mrs. (Jeanne) Henrie Cyr, Henrie Cyr, Mrs. Eric Ouellette, Eric Ouellette, Mrs. (Alma) Levite Cyr, and Levite Cyr. Such anniversaries are extremely important in the family-structured life of the Valley.

14

Mrs. Alexis Dufour and her seven daughters in 1940 at St. David (part of Madawaska). From left to right are Rose, Albertine, Annie, Mrs. Dufour (Leonie Cyr), Catherine, Marie, Helen, and Lucie. Large families are common in the Valley. The largest family in this region I have known included 32 children and the parents.

Israel and Ernest Smart of Eagle Lake in a 1906 photograph that cost 20¢. The picture was taken by a traveling photographer. Chairs and backgrounds were set up at the local Catholic church. Family photographs of any kind were always an event.

15

The Louis and Agnes (Powers) Dionne family, c. 1920s, in Van Buren. From left to right are as follows: (sitting) Louis and Agnes Dionne; (standing) Rose (Mrs. John Pelletier), Everett Dionne, Catherine (Mrs. Philip Gagnon), Wilfred Dionne, Leroy Dionne, and Henrietta Dionne.

Ozelie Thibodeau and Alma Pelletier, c. 1930s. Alma married Levite Thibodeau (right), who lived next door to the Pelletiers in Van Buren.

Children of Joseph Dufour of St. Agatha, c. 1910s. The Dufours were most probably a farm family. The role of the children was very important in running and maintaining Valley farms because they provided a large part of the labor. With school and farm chores, a child did not have much time for leisure activities.

The Despres family at Eagle Lake in the early 1900s. They are, from left to right, as follows: (front) Michael and Alexander Despres; (back) Delia Michaud (who was brought up by the Despres uncles after she arrived from the orphan train), Ella Labbe (a cousin of the Despres), Catherine Raymond; and ? Nadeau. Well-off families took care of orphans whenever possible.

Paul Thibodeau of St. Francis, c. 1900. Born in 1850, Paul was quite prominent in St. Francis, which lies between Fort Kent and Allagash on the St. John. Like the Thibodeaus, other families, such as the Cyrs, the Dufours, the Alberts, and the Daigles, spread along the Valley through marriage.

Joe Thibodeau and his wife, Sophie Lavoie, at Grand Isle, October 1, 1905. Grand Isle is another of the towns between Van Buren and Madawaska on the St. John. Reports indicate that this branch of the Thibodeaus left the area, as did many, especially during the Depression.

Wedding picture of Albert and Annie (Cyr) Thibodeau, who were married June 22, 1903, at Fort Kent.

The Paul D. Thibodeau family in Fort Kent, c. 1930. Paul D. may have been the son of Paul Thibodeau of St. Francis, who later moved to Fort Kent. The latter was a state legislator.

Joe Thibodeau and his wife, Philomene Freeman, of Fort Kent, and their grandson, Miles "Cookie" Pelletier. Joe and Philomene were married in Eagle Lake on April 5, 1908. This photograph was taken in 1934. Joe Thibodeau was at one time a Fort Kent road commissioner.

Children of Mr. and Mrs. Joe Thibodeau of Fort Kent, c. 1925. They are, from left to right, as follows: (seated) unidentified and George; (middle row) Pauline, Dorin, and Lawrence; (back row) Corrine and Nat.

Mrs. (Marie Audibert) Alvarez
Thibodeau of Fort Kent.

Hugh Thibodeau (1863–1925) and his first wife, Ozithe (Zithe) Violette (1870–1905). They were married in Van Buren, February 26, 1889, and lived in Grand Isle. Hugh Thibodeau is remembered as a very large man and as a very "colorful character" of the area.

Betsie (Elizabeth) Thibodeau of St. Francis, born in 1862. Her granddaughter, Kathleen Berube, is on the right, and her husband is in the center of this *c.* 1920s photograph.

Maxime and Jane Thibodeau (he was oldest son of Mathiase Thibodeau), married in St. Francis, *c.* 1900s.

Hotel Dieu Hospital in Van Buren, c. 1920s. The hospital was first the residence of Attorney L.V. Thibodeau and Ozelie Thibodeau, and became a store after its hospital days were over.

The George Madore family of Van Buren. From left to right they are as follows: (front row) John Madore, Mrs. (Marie) George Madore, Armand Madore, George Madore (the father), and Eldridge Madore; (back row) Clifford and Guy Madore.

John B. Pelletier and Rose (Dionne) Pelletier, parents of Martine A. Pelletier, who was the co-author of the pictorial history of Van Buren.

Wilfred Dufour, son of Belonie Dufour of St. Agatha, 1915. He owned and operated a general store in St. Agatha.

24

The Michel Dufour family of
St. Agatha in 1900. Michael
was a tinsmith.

The Belonie Dufour family
in St. Agatha in the 1920s.
Belonie Dufour was a farmer
in the area.

The family of Paul Lagasse Dufour and his wife, Susanne, in St. Agatha, c. 1900. They are, from left to right, as follows: (middle row) Marie Chasse, Susanne Lagasse, Beatrice Dufour Derosier, Alice Cyr Dufour (wife of Belonie), Lucie Dufour Hebert, and Marie Dufour Dube (a teacher and superintendent of schools in Castine); (back row) Paul (a farmer), Maxime Derosier (a son-in-law who lived in Keegan), Belonie (a farmer), William (a farmer), and Albert Hebert (a son-in-law and a barber in St. Agatha and Madawaska). The children, not in order, are Bertrand Dufour (who later worked for Champion Paper in Lawrence, MA), Bertha Dufour Pelletier; Lucien Chasse (now a retired priest in Boston), Juliette Chasse, and an unidentified girl.

Little Mildred L. Daigle, c. 1920, the daughter of Josephel Daigle of St. Agatha.

Mirance Belanger (right), c. 1910, at Wallagrass or Eagle Lake. Phoebe McGlauflin (left) was Mirance's daughter, and Grace McGlauflin is in the center. The baby's name is unknown, but this was a four-generation photograph.

Modeste Madore, the great aunt of Lewellyn Despres, at Eagle Lake in the 1940s.

A good-looking Rolande Despres, age 23, in 1942, at Eagle Lake.

Rolande Despres of Eagle Lake at her 1942 marriage to Eric Brandt, a native of Sweden.

Rolda Despres, Rolande's sister, in 1942.

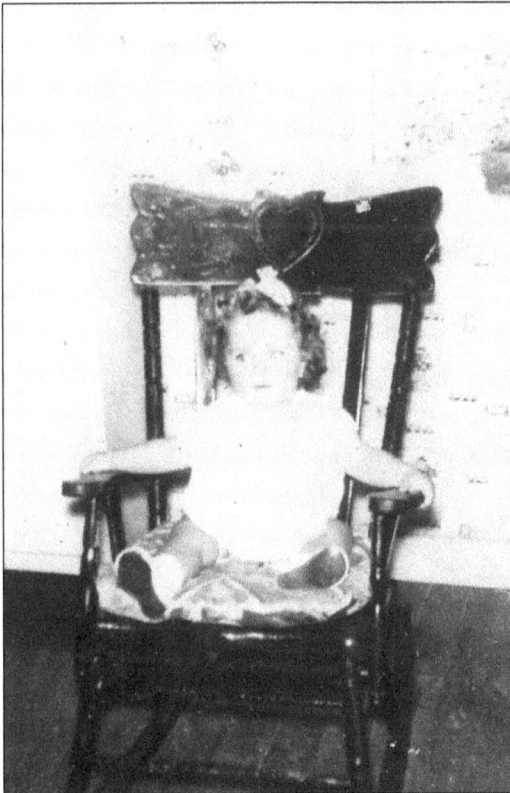

Linda Belanger in 1947 or 1948 at Eagle Lake. Linda was the daughter of Rose Belanger, and she died in January 1994.

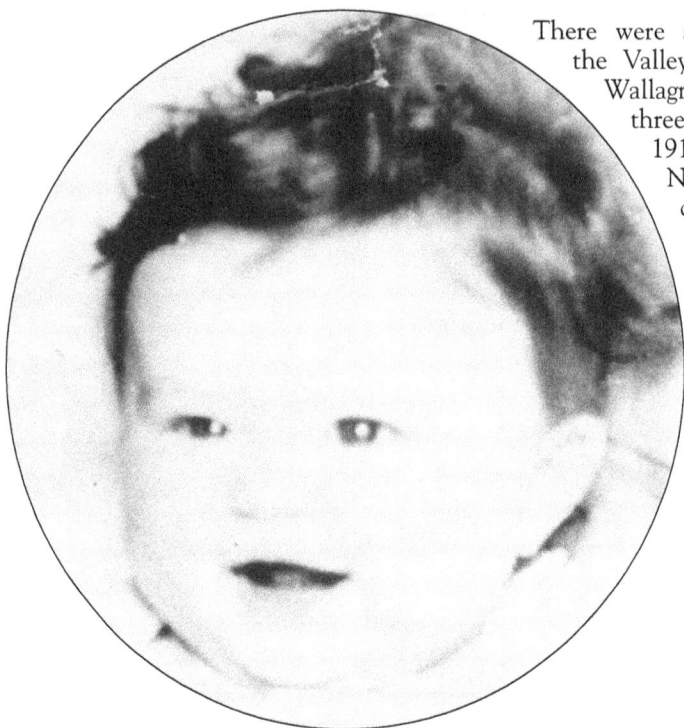

There were sad sides to family life in the Valley. Elucide Saucier, son of a Wallagrass farmer, died at the age of three from Spanish influenza in 1918. From early October to late November that year, over 40 deaths were recorded in the general area of Eagle Lake and Wallagrass.

Last gathering at the old homestead in October 1959 at Madawaska. Mr. and Mrs. Eloi Lavoie sit with their family at their 109-year-old house, where all the children were born. The house was torn down the week after this photograph was taken. They are, from left to right, as follows: (front row) Felix, Mr. Lavoie, Mrs. (Laura Martin) Lavoie, and Louise (Mrs. Ernest Ruest); (back row) Cecile (Mrs. Telesphore Raymond), Martin, Aurore (Mrs. Antoine Damour), Robert, and Lorraine (Mrs. Jean Luke Picard).

Three

Farms

Bringing in hay to be unloaded in the barn. Women and children often helped with such chores.

Spraying potatoes in the summer of 1920. At the far right is Fred Albert, the son of Laurent.

Picking potatoes at John McElwee's farm in Caribou in 1927. Such scenes were common all over the Valley at this time, though Caribou is about 20 miles to the south. Potatoes became the Valley's prime crop in the late nineteenth century. Since World War II, there has been a sharp decline in such Valley farms.

First tractor at the Joseph Marquis farm in 1930. Seen here with Marquis is Annie Cyr (Mrs. Lewis Cote). This farm was located in the Birch Point section of Madawaska.

Harvesting buckwheat in 1949 on the Cyr farm in Madawaska. Seen in this photograph are Laurent Cyr (left), Remi (in the jeep), and Alvin Cyr (driving the tractor). Buckwheat is one of the principal ingredients of *ployes*, the Valley's famous pancake-like food.

33

Winter photograph of the barnyard at Thadée Theriault's farm in the early 1920s in St. David.

Fred Lagasse, age 65, in 1937. Fred is preparing a noon-time meal of fried salt pork and eggs and taking a break from cutting wood for winter fuel in the fall on his farm next to the St. David Church. This was, of course, in the depths of the Depression.

A view of the unique log house on Abel Picard's farm in Madawaska. The first owner of that farm was either Remi or Frank Hebert.

A Fort Kent barn. Barns came in many shapes and sizes in the Valley.

The Daigle & Sons barn in Fort Kent.

I.L. Cyr's potato house. There are or have been similar houses all over Aroostook County.

St. David farms, south of the church there. St. David was once the busiest part of Madawaska but has been considerably less busy since the Fraser Paper mill was built north of that area. In the foreground is the John J. Cyr farm; the Vilas Picard farm is in the center with what was then the Adolphe Hebert farm. The latter farm was later owned by Daniel Cyr, Mrs. Michel Picard, and Emile Hebert.

A brand new barn! This 1914 photograph shows, from left to right, Vilas, Xavier, unidentified, Fred, Leonard, and Felix, all sons of Ubald Dufour. The barn was in St. David.

Turkey raising in
Grand Isle, 1949. Dave
Vaillancourt ushers
his herd outside for its
breakfast and morning
exercises.

Alred Vaillancourt of Fort Kent in the
1890s or early 1900s. He was a small
farmer and a trapper, especially of beaver.

The Despres farmstead at Eagle Lake in the early 1940s.

Joel, Simone, Michel (the father), and
Rolda Despres at their Eagle Lake farm,
c. 1940.

Raymond (Bee) Despres's truck in front of the Michel Hebert farm at Eagle Lake.

Raymond (Bee) Despres in front of
the Michel Hebert farm in Eagle Lake,
c. 1940s.

Four

Religion

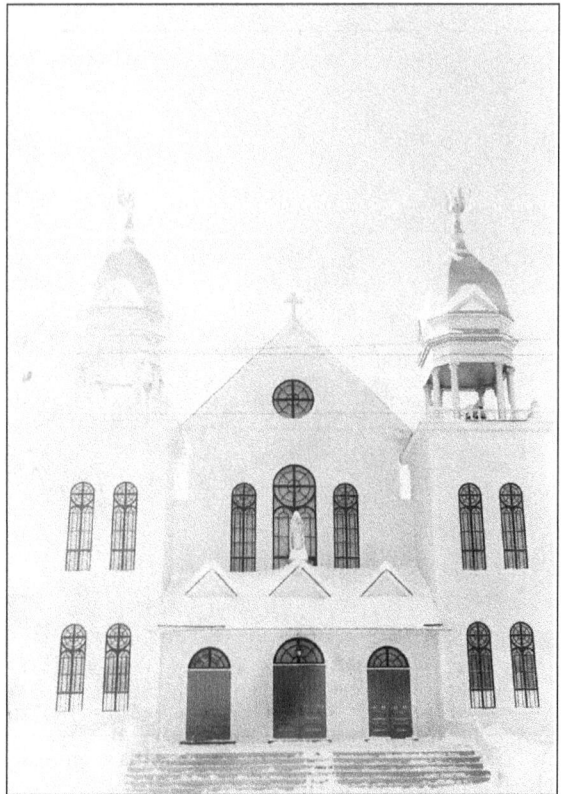

Notre Dame du Mont-Carmel, Lille, listed in the National Register of Historic Places in 1973. It was closed September 18, 1977, and is now L'Association Culturelle Et Historique du Mont-Carmel. This former church is of the old style. The statues atop each tower are of the Archangels Michael and Gabriel. Seven feet high, they were carved by Louis Jobin of Ste-Anne de Beaupre, Quebec, about 1908–1909, according to J. Donald Cyr, association president. The lower statue is of Notre Dame du Mont-Carmel.

St. Gerard Church, Grand Isle, in 1931. The church is now St. Gerard-Notre Dame du Mont Carmel. The strength of the Catholic religion in the Valley is as great as ever.

St. Louis Church, Fort Kent, c. 1950. This is quite an impressive edifice even without its tower, which is not visible in this photograph.

The first St. David Church in Madawaska. When this structure was built, St. David was the commercial center of Madawaska. It is also the area where the first Acadians landed from the St. John in 1785 and permanently settled.

The New Church of St. David, Me.
Rev. L. E. Huot, Pastor.

Reverend L.E. Huot, pastor from 1907 to 1918, who had the present St. David Church built.

St. Thomas Aquinas Church and School in Madawaska. The building on the right in 1929 housed the church on the first floor and the school on the second. In 1939 the church in the center was built. The school building is now the Madawaska Out Patient Center.

First convent of Wallagrass, opened by Father Fondateur in 1898.

First St. Michael Chapel at Long Lake (Birch Point) in 1950. It was a mission of St. Agatha Parish. The building was originally a dance hall.

St. Agatha Church and Convent, c. 1907. Note how its size and impressive edifice dominates the town.

St. Agatha Convent of the Daughters of Wisdom. Built in 1904, the convent was demolished in 1968. It had a barracks-like appearance with its four stories.

Second St. Agatha Church, c. 1940. The church's building is more modern with a smaller tower and appears more like a traditional New England church.

The third church at Frenchville (between Madawaska and Fort Kent on the St. John) in 1907. This is closer to the typical New England church.

First St. Bruno Church in Van Buren in 1871. Note the tall steeple and the two side towers.

Good Shepherd Convent, Van Buren, built for the Reverend Paul Ralquien, S.M., in 1919.

Une famile religieuse. Patrick V. Beaulieu (left) poses with daughter Nancy and his wife in the back seat of a car driven by Uncle Sylvio Lizotte. In this 1931 photograph, his daughters, Sisters Irene, Claire, and Annette, stand on the right. On the running board of the car are Mrs. (Marie Lizotte) Denis Daigle of St. Basile, New Brunswick, and Una and Hedwidge Lizotte. Una later entered the Order of the Little Sisters of the Holy Family with her three sisters. There were other Valley families that had a majority of their children become priests and nuns.

St. John Valley Council, 2638, Knights of Columbus, in a *c.* 1940 parade in Madawaska. The Knights of Columbus, of course, is very strong in the Valley.

Rev. Pierre-Paul Dufour, son of Narcisse Dufour, and Sister Jeanne Mance (Emma Dufour), daughter of Ubald Dufour. He was Sister Jeanne Mance's uncle. Father Dufour was ordained August 10, 1891, at Saint John, New Brunswick. He was first a secular priest and later joined the Congregation of the Priests of the Holy Cross. For many years, he was chaplain at the provincial penitentiary in Dorchester, New Brunswick. Sister Mance was a member of the cloistered nuns, Hospitaliers of St. Joseph. A teacher before she became a nun, Sister Mance also taught and worked as a nurse while a nun. Both Reverend Dufour and Sister Mance were Madawaska natives.

Rev. Euloge LaPlante, S.M., born in Van Buren on April 1, 1913. He professed his religious beliefs in the Society of Mary on September 5, 1934, and was later ordained February 24, 1942. Father LaPlante died July 16, 1983.

Msg. L.N. Dugal in a photograph taken May 27, 1926. He died in St. Basile, New Brunswick, across the St. John River from the St. David section of Madawaska on November 27, 1929. Revered by all, Monseigneur Dugal had become a priest in St. Basile in 1871 and became vicar-general in 1880.

Rev. Charles Sweron, born in Weert, Belgium, and buried in St. Luce cemetery, Upper Frenchville, where he had been the priest at St. Luce Church from 1859 until his death. He first came to the Valley in 1857 as a priest at St. Francis. An able administrator, Father Sweron also served St. David in Madawaska from 1871 to 1881; Notre Dame du Mont Carmel, Lille (part of Grand Isle), from 1876 to 1880; St. Agatha's mission until 1889; and the Sacred Heart mission in North Caribou in 1875. In 1898, he established the convent school at St. Luce, turning it over to the Holy Rosary Sisters of Rimooski, Quebec.

St. David Church confirmation class in the 1920s.

Five

Education

The Class of 1905–1906 at the Madawaska Training School, Fort Kent, forerunner of the University of Maine at Fort Kent. Among those in the picture are Olive Cyr, Flavie A. Cyr, Jean A. Cyr, Lizzie Anne V. Cyr, and Annie Picard, all of St. David-Madawaska; and Catherine Bouchard and Pete Roy of Frenchville. My grandmother, then Cora Carpenter (later Putnam) of Houlton, went to the training school from 1887 to 1890. That first year, 1887, was the first permanent settlement of the school in Fort Kent. It had previously alternated terms in Van Buren and Fort Kent.

Madawaska Training School graduates, 1908. They are, from left to right, as follows: (seated) Catherine Dufour and Albertine Nadeau; (standing) Laura Cyr, Annie Cyr, Louise Daigle, and Agnes Daigle. When the school first started, it had three years (the equivalent of high school) and one year of teacher training, with an emphasis on Classical education. My grandmother taught for several years in the Valley after she graduated.

St. David cousins who attended the Madawaska Training School at Fort Kent for two years, c. 1908. They are, from left to right, as follows: (front row) Thomas Pelletier, Carolyn LeBrun, Anna Pelletier, and Louise Dufour; (middle row) Carolyne Dufour, Annie Dufour, and Laura Cyr; (back row) Eddie Cyr, Annie Cyr, Helen Pelletier, Emelia Cyr, and Levite Dufour.

Class of 1908, the Madawaska Training School, with Principal Mary Nowland. The graduates shown here include Luc Albert, Demond J. Cyr, Lizzie Cyr, Rex Dow, Caroline Dufour, Catherine Dufour, Louise Dufour, Agnes Lang, Helene Lang, Nellie McDonald, Myra Mullen, Joseph Nadeau, Uphemie Pelletier, and Euphemic Roy.

Class of 1915, the Madawaska Training School, Fort Kent. These students are, from left to right, as follows: (front row) Yvonne Michaud, Gertrude Albert, Lizzie Anne Brown, Emma Pinette, Carrie Bolstridae, Madeline Cyr, and Marie Nadeau; (middle row) Frank Eaton, Irene L'Abbe, Laura Pelletier, Irene Daigle, Emelie Dionne, Ida L'Abbe, Alice Cyr, Stella Freeman, and Madeline Boulier; (back row) Delima Cyr, George Pelletier, Rose St. John, Aurore Roy, Annie Marie Bellefleur, Dieudonne Long, and Julia Raymond.

Miss Mary Nowland (left), principal of the Madawaska Training School, and Miss Doon, a teacher there, *c*. 1920.

The first class of boys at the Madawaska Training School, 1920.

Marie Dufour (Mrs. Henry Dube), who lived from 1899 to 1979. She was a schoolteacher and later superintendent of schools in School Union 127. Mrs. Dube was the daughter of Paul Dufour of St. Agatha.

Schoolteacher Catherine Albert, who later became principal of Evangeline School, Madawaska.

Madawaska High School teachers in 1937. They are pictured in front of what was the Acadia School. The teachers are, from left to right, as follows: (front row) Evelyn Jalbert (twelfth grade), Priscilla Beland, Principal Ralph Foster, Virginia Nadeau, and Lenora Michaud; (back row) Joseph O'Toole, Eleanor Connor, Mary Crowley, and Thomas Crowley.

Class of 1937, the Madawaska High School. The students are, from left to right, as follows: (front row) Cecile Dufour, Theresa Dufour, Martha Picard, Aurore Cyr, Irene Martin, and unknown; (middle row) Alcide Hebert, Alice Dionne, Margaret Noel, Gilbert Fongemie, Ruth Reed, Rita Michaud, and class advisor Miss Evelyn Jalbert; (back row) Hector Dionne, Camille Caron, Louis Fournier, Reno Daigle, Arthur Daigle, Truman Messecar, Normand Fournier, and Paul Clavette.

58

Patrick Theriault, superintendent of schools, c. 1920, for Lille, Grand Isle, St. Agatha, Frenchville, and Sinclair. He later was both a state representative, state senator, and an Aroostook County Commissioner.

Madawaska High School Owl Staff, 1940. They are, from left to right, as follows: (front row) R. Bouchard, M.L. Dufour, J. Cyr, T. Cyr, O. King, A. Collins, L. Carrier, B. Soucy, and M. Dionne; (back row) adviser Miss Morneault, H. Gerard, N. Pelletier. L. Goodwin, J.L. Tardif, P. Martin, M. Garon, B. Spicer, R. Dufour, R. White, and advisor Mr. Fox.

59

The Civilian Conservation Corps (CCC) camp in Winter Harbor, Maine. The CCC was important all over Maine in the 1930s. Here we see Raymond Despres (left) and Rene Michaud of Eagle Lake at the CCC camp.

St. Mary's College, Van Buren, in 1907. The school lasted longer than the short-lived John F. Kennedy College in modern Fort Kent did, but it faded away some decades ago.

Six

Business

Crawford Lumber Mill, in Grand Isle, which burned to the ground in July 1913. Farming and industries involving the forest were the two principal income producers of the Valley for years.

St. John Lumber Co., Keegan (next to Van Buren and a part of that town), *c.* 1920s.

The Charles Lacroix lumber mill, Notre Dame, Lille (part of Grand Isle). The company moved to Keegan in the early 1920s. In the foreground is Elias Poirier (now deceased), father of Mrs. Lawrence Savoie Sr., of Madawaska

The plant of the St. John Lumber Co. in Van Buren, c. 1920s.

Ford garage and the Yesbec Building, Madawaska, in 1926. On the far right is the bunkhouse-dining hall owned by Arthur J. Daigle, which he operated during the lumbering work. The Ford garage was owned by Edmund J. Cyr. On the first floor of the Charles Yesbec Building were Boston Clothing Store (left), owned by Levi Klein with Jim Cyr, clerk; the Parisienne Ladies Shop (right), owned by Mrs. Edmund J. Cyr with Birdie LaChance (Mayhew), clerk; and the first telephone office (upstairs), with Mrs. Minnie Cyr as the first operator. Later, the clothing stores were replaced by the post office and the Golden Lion Restaurant.

Young men at a Valley lumber camp before World War I. These workers are, from left to right, as follows: (front row) Fortunat Rossignol, Thomas O. Cyr, and Ernest O. Cyr; (back row) Henry Lagasse, Levite M. Cyr, Henery Beaulieu, and Emmanuel Picard. The American Legion post in Madawaska is named in honor of Thomas O. Cyr, who was killed in World War I.

Getting ready for construction of the Fraser Paper mill in Madawaska, May 30, 1925. The Fraser Paper mill completely changed the economic structure of the town. Note the first customhouse near the bridge; it was built in 1923.

The completed Fraser Paper Ltd. mill, October 3, 1925.

Fifteenth Avenue in Madawaska. The bungalows were built by Fraser Paper for employees in 1926. The construction of employee housing was one vital part of the way Fraser changed the entire economy of Madawaska.

Aerial view of Madawaska and Edmundston, New Brunswick, in the early 1940s, showing both Fraser Paper mills in operation.

Fraser constantly expanded, as this 1956 photograph shows.

Weighing rolls of paper for shipping in Fraser Paper's bond shipping room at the Madawaska mill. The company's paper goes all over the United States and Canada as well as to foreign countries.

Groundwood save-all at the Fraser Paper catalog mill in 1957. Joe Boucher is visible in this photograph. Note the symmetry of the paper mill machinery.

Pulp mill in Keegan, c. 1900s.

Maine game wardens did other work during
their off-duty hours. Here, Warden Harold Dow
scales logs in 1932 for resident Jim Martin's
camp on the Allagash. Valley farmers, especially
during the Depression, worked in the woods
during the winters.

A.E. Hammonds's new lumber mill on Violette Brook, Van Buren, in 1916. The lumber mill
burned in 1918.

Madawaska Lumber Company mill in Keegan, c. 1900. The Van Buren–Keegan area once flourished more than it does now.

Reynold Despres in front of the Eagle Lake bowling pin mill in 1951.

The Van Buren gristmill, usually owned and operated by the Violette family. This particular mill, built in 1826, continued operating into the 1950s.

Isabelle Michaud of Eagle Lake at the original corner store during World War II. She is holding her daughter Nancy.

The Dufour general store in St. Agatha, c. 1929. Pierre Paul Dufour, son of Belonie Dufour, is seen along with Arm & Hammer products on one shelf and Thrift Seeded Raisins on another.

Joe Cyr's grocery store, Grand Isle, now Gordon Soucy's grocery store, c. 1910s.

Wilfred Plourde, Alcide Tardif, and John J. Plourde (father) in Plourde's IGA Store, Van Buren, c. 1920s.

Grand Isle Hotel, Mrs. Vital (Annie) Thibodeau's rooming house, c. 1910s.

Al Gioux (left) and Ernest Smart. The two men operated a sugar camp at the foot of Hog Mountain, near Winterville, in the 1940s. Also at the camp were members of the Michaud, Vaillancourt, and Tardie families.

Jim Hafford, Rob Hafford, and Hazen Taggett, among others, in Allagash with a log hauler.

Seven

Towns

A 1936 view of Main Street, Madawaska, filled with many cars. The paper mill did well in spite of the Depression.

Fred Beaulieu's Lunch Room, Main Street, Grand Isle, *c.* 1910.

Main Street, Keegan, *c.* 1920s. This section of Van Buren was named after prominent businessman Patrick Keegan.

Main Street, Van Buren, *c.* 1900. Note the E. Lebrun store.

Main Street, Van Buren, *c.* 1900. Stores included Michael S. Harris, a tailor and clothier with "cleaning, pressing, and repairing," a restaurant next door, and F.O. Michaud (farther down the street).

Main Street, Van Buren, in the 1940s with the Hotel Van Buren visible. There had been a lot of change over the years.

Post office, Van Buren, c. 1920s.

Station Street, Keegan, *c*. 1920s.

Notre Dame railroad station in Lille, *c*. 1910s. The station was named after the parish of Notre Dame du Mont Carmel.

Grand Isle railroad station in 1911. A train is waiting.

Van Buren railroad station, c. 1910s.

A train moving along the side of Eagle Lake in the 1950s in Plaisted. This photograph was taken from Route 11 by Walter Wallerman, a professional photographer from Clinton, Massachusetts, who came from Eagle Lake. This picture gives some idea of the area's scenic beauty. The arrival of the Bangor & Aroostook Railroad opened the Valley to larger crop, lumber, and paper production.

State Senator Patrick Theriault's home in Lille. The house was located across from the Lille church, c. 1910s.

Residence and garage of Charlie Violette in Lille, *c*. 1930.

Charlie Violette in front of his house in Lille, sitting on the running board of his car, *c*. 1920.

Residence of Hypolite Cote on P'tite Montagne Road, St. David. Seen in this 1913 photograph are, from left to right, Donat Cote; Emelida Cote (Mrs. George Thibodeau); Mrs. Cote (Euphemie Levesque), first wife; Catherine Cote Bechard, niece; Henri Cote; Eloi Cote; and Hypolite Cote.

Come-Gerard Beaulieu house in St. David.

Fort Kent customhouse, 1930. From left to right are Frank Ford, Ernest Coltart, Emile Bourgoin, Charlie Crawford, Edward Daigle, and Eddie Doyle (on the motorcycle).

Customhouse workers in Fort Kent, c. 1930. These men are, from left to right, Immigration Inspector Fred Bouchard, Custom Inspector Sanborn, and Patrol Inspector Ernest Coltart.

Ernest Coltart, immigration officer, going to work on snowshoes at Fort Kent in the early 1930s. This area is part of the longest unguarded frontier in the world.

Fort Kent flood, May 10, 1939, on Main Street. Dr. Page is the farthest left of the three men on the raft in the foreground.

Thomas Dufour's 1930 Ford, seen moving along Lavertu Road in the back settlement of Madawaska during the winter of 1935. Dufour was working for the soil conservation people.

First ambulance in Madawaska, 1935. This hearse was used as an ambulance. The sign hanging from the porch reads as follows: "E.A. Daigle, undertaker, tel 2-13."

Aerial view of St. Agatha, 1954.

Another view of Eagle Lake's beauty from Route 11 in the 1950s.

Northern Maine Hospital, Eagle Lake Mills, with windmill, c. 1910. The hospital was opened in 1905 by the Little Franciscan Sisters of Mary of Baie St. Paul, Quebec.

Northern Maine Hospital, Eagle Lake, c. 1920s, without the windmill. The Little Franciscan Sisters left in 1966, and the Sisters of Mercy took over in 1968. Under the Sisters of Mercy, the facility became more of a long-term care hospital.

War hero. Every Valley town, it seems, has its war heroes. Patrick O. Corbin, the son of Mr. and Mrs. Abel Corbin of Lille, was killed in active duty in France on July 26, 1944, at the age of 19 years and 11 months.

Patrick Morneault, born in Lille on March 6, 1928. Patrick was killed in Korea on July 27, 1953, at the age of 25.

A LA DOUCE MÉMOIRE DE

VICTORIE GENDREAULT

Fils de Raymond Gendreault

Mort en France, le 4 novembre 1918,
à l'âge de 26 ans.

Mourir pour la patrie, c'est mourir pour Dieu espérons qu'il est allé cueillir là-haut les lauriers de la victoire, car sur sa fosse encore entrouverte la paix et la justice se sent entrebaisées, son sang généreusement versé nous a mérité l'ère de liberté dont nous jouissons.

"In sweet memory of Victorie Gendreault, dead in France, November 4, 1918, at the age of 26. To die for your country is to die for God . . ."

Missionary Cross in Keegan, *c.* 1920.

Eight

Allagash Minority

A ferry across the Allagash River in Allagash, close to where the Allagash flows into the St. John, *c.* 1934.

A ferry moving over the St. John at Allagash in 1944. The car on the ferry was one of the few automobiles in the town at that time. There was no real road there and school was closed from December to March, largely because of transport problems.

Pulp jam in the Little Black River, Allagash. The Little Black runs into the St. John at Dickey, just west of Allagash.

Driving logs for Irving Paper Co. in the St. John River at Allagash. This was the last log drive in the river, 1960. The Scotch-Irish community makes its living from the woods. There are not many farms now.

Painting of the covered bridge over the Little Black River in Allagash or Dickey. The bridge was destroyed in the 1970s.

A log landing on the Allagash River, Allagash, about 1937. Visible in the picture are, not in order, Faye O'Leary (Hafford), Belle Gardner, Beatrice O'Leary, and Parker Henderson.

A tow boat on the St. John River at Allagash on July 4, 1922. Before there were good roads, these boats were often used to bring supplies to the town.

Log jam at Cross Rock in Allagash on the St. John River in the 1930s. This place was the site of a proposed hydroelectric power dam project in the 1960s and 1970s, as was the Dickey-Lincoln School section of the Upper St. John. Nothing ever worked out.

Alex Moir in front of his house at Cross Rock in the town of Allagash and on the St. John River in the 1930s. One of his sons, Jonathan, had an "s" stuck on his last name on his Christening certificate. The extra letter stayed, and another son, Charlie, had it on his wedding certificate.

The Moir garden at the family homestead at Cross Rock, Allagash, by the St. John River. Jonathan Moirs is walking on the road in the background. There were hand-made shingles on the farm. The house later burned, but a new one was built. This picture might have been taken in the 1930s.

Belle Moirs Sullivan, standing at the rear in this 1930s photograph behind her parents, Alex and Anne Gardner Moir, in front of the family homestead at Allagash. Alex Moir is said to have been born in a canoe on the St. John as the family migrated from the Campbellton area of New Brunswick.

Dawn Moirs (center) in 1932 with Ernest (left) and Guy (right). Did she shoot the deer?

An old schoolhouse. The building on the left in this December 1941 photograph was first a home on the St. Francis-Allagash town line and then a storage shed by the Moirs' Cross Rock home. It was eventually sold to the Town of Allagash to be a schoolhouse, and the last classes in it were in the fall of 1923.

A car seen on the ice of the Allagash River in Allagash in 1944. Faye O'Leary is on the left and her sister Beatrice is on the right.

Jim Hafford (right), 1950s. He cooked at many different lumber camps. He is shown here with Clayton Grenier (left) and Leon Wardwell.

Lester Gardner in 1947 on the Allagash River in Allagash with an old motor in his boat. Many Allagash men and some women are registered Maine guides. Lester was guiding at McNally's when this was taken.

Joseph O'Leary of Allagash in his World War I uniform. Note the predominance of Irish and English names so far in Allagash, a contrast to the French names in the rest of the Upper St. John Valley.

Jim Merritt (left) of Fort Fairfield with Calvin O'Leary (center) and Elbert O'Leary of Allagash. These men are cooking their dinner at the foot of Allagash Falls before World War II. Cal was wounded in the war.

Guides and wardens. Those in this 1910s photograph are, from left to right, as follows: (front) famed Maine guide and warden baiter Sam Jalbert of Fort Kent and Dennis Pelletier, who guided the Allagash ferry for years; (rear) Tom Pelletier, Lee Gardner, and Alvey Casey.

The first bus in Allagash. The bus, seen here on Inn Road, Allagash, was operated by L.E. "Lull" Pelletier from Allagash to Fort Kent during World War II. After the war ended, so did the bus.

Randi Hafford (Jandreau) at the age of three by Lull's Store (L.E. Pelletier). Randi later became a teacher.

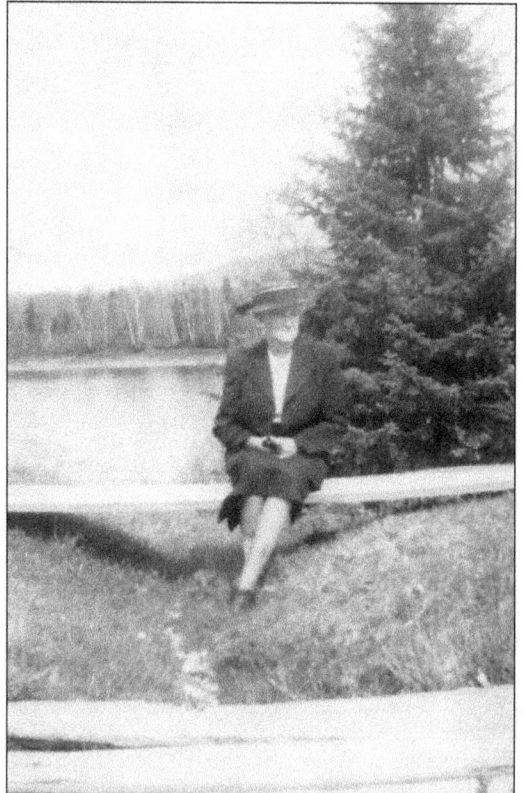

Gladys Gardner, a teacher, on the Allagash River in Allagash near her home in the early 1950s.

Nine

Leisure Time and Recreation

St. Agatha gathering for fun, probably in the 1930s. These people are, from left to right, as follows: (front row) Edith Albert, Patrick Albert, Maxime Lagasse, Pegete Michaud, another Maxime Lagasse?, and unidentified; (middle row) Joseph Lagasse, Henriette Dubois, Caron Lagasse, Marguerite Lagasse, and Paul Dufour; (back row) William Dufour, Amanda Cyr Dufour, Albert Hebert, Lucie Dufour Hebert, unidentified, Alice Cyr Dufour, Tazie Lagasse Albert, and Belonie Dufour.

Mr. and Mrs. Magloire Collin (Caroline Dionne). This pair was married at St. Agatha June 23, 1900, by Rev. H. Gori. This photograph was taken when fur coats were in style in the 1920s.

Semi-pro baseball player Alvie Lebrun, husband of Louise Dufour, at Van Buren, c. 1910.

Waiting to give airplane rides in Madawaska on a Sunday afternoon in 1923. Not enough emphasis has been placed on the fact that Valley people, in spite of all their hard work and strenuous survival conditions, do like a good time.

A float in the 1927 Labor Day Parade in Madawaska. The float, which won first prize, was sponsored by Local 247 of the International Brotherhood of Paper Makers. Bernadette Lachance (Mayhew), representing the Parisienne Shop in Madawaska, was the driver.

Lucien A. Cyr of Madawaska and his prime catch. Lucien caught the 21-pound, 1-ounce landlocked salmon at Birch Point, Long Lake, June 14, 1941.

Donat and Aline Dufour of St. David on the rear bumper of their father's car, 1931.

Madawaska High School cheerleaders, 1947–48. They are, from left to right, Mavis Comstock (Michaud), Betty Labbe (Jessome), Margaret Duthie, Rachel Gerard, Connie Mayhew (Joyce), Mary Mavor, and Patsy Dufour. Miss Feeney, the coach, is standing in the rear.

Madawaska High School first boys' and girls' basketball team, 1933–34. There were no uniforms and no gym. They played on the second floor of Daigle's Drug Store. They are, from left to right, as follows: (front row) Francis McDermott, Austin Wylie, and Conde Picard; (second row) Ruth Reed, Lorraine McDermott, Eloise Cyr, and Adeline Gerard; (third row) Bernice Dufour, Lorraine Dufour, and Isabel Bourgoin; (back row) Armand Guerrette, Alfred (Freddie) Fournier, and Raynaldo Dufour.

Madawaska High School's 1948 Aroostook County track champions. They are, from left to right, as follows: (sitting) Gerald Dufour, Real Grandmaison, Buddy MacMahon, and Dick Mayhew; (standing) Coach Miles Murphy, Cliff Madore, Norman Leblanc, and Robert Sirois.

The first Madawaska High School Winter Carnival Queen, Ruth Reed, on February 24, 1934.

The 1959 Soap Box Derby in Brewer with Number 43, Guy Martin of Madawaska, winning.

St. John Valley Fairgrounds in 1940 in front of I.L. Cyr's potato houses.

Hunting, mid-1940s. Hanging from a proud hunter's gun, these four oversized partridges were shot by Damase Smart of Eagle Lake during a hunting trip when he was 87 years old.

Father and daughter, Ernest and Christie Smart, in 1952. They were inspecting the Fort Kent blockhouse; the fort was in poor shape then but has since been restored.

Reminiscent of Thoreau? This group canoeing the Allagash River on a fishing trip in 1926 included Hal and Nora Dow and a friend.

The Van Buren Cornet Band of 1902. They are, from left to right, as follows: (front row) three unknowns and Eddie Martin; (middle row) William Scott, Joseph A. Violette, unidentified, Slyvail Beaulieu, Guy S. Cyr, Reno Albert, and Tim Beaudrea; (back row) Johnny Cyr, Emery Theriault, Philip Gagnon, Luke Albert, Joseph Boudreau, and Cyprien Caron.

The 1933–34 Van Buren High School basketball team. The coach was Bill Lynch (right, back row). The players include Bob Marquis, Rosaire Dubois, Claude Lebel, Benoit Picard, Charlie Pelletier, Lawrence Soucy, Clifford Parent, Leonice Martin, Alyce Dumon, Val Violette, Alderic Violette, and Alphonse Dubay..

Van Buren baseball team, c. 1900. They are, from left to right, as follows: (front row) Rene Violette and Everett Dionne; (middle row) Edward Michaud, Eugene Lebrun, Pat Violette, Albert Madore, and Mo Violette; (back row) Joseph Violette, Joseph Michaud, Theophile Violette, and Arthur Dionne.

Joseph and Levite Vaillancourt of Eagle Lake enjoying a small nip, *c.* 1890s.

Eighth graders from Dirigo School, Eagle Lake. The class has just finished clearing an outdoor skating area in 1949.

Michel Despres in 1942 at Winterville with a World War I cannon assembled in the 1930s by George Morin.

Michel Despres in 1952 at St. Froid Lake, south of Eagle Lake, with his granddaughter, Wanda Wallerman, and fish.

Ten

Doers and Shakers

Thomas Thibodeau, pioneer
settler of Fort Kent, *c.* 1860.

Elie Thibodeau (1828–1908), first settler of St. Francis, *c.* 1900. He married Seconde Jalbert (1829–1910) at St. Luce Church, Frenchville.

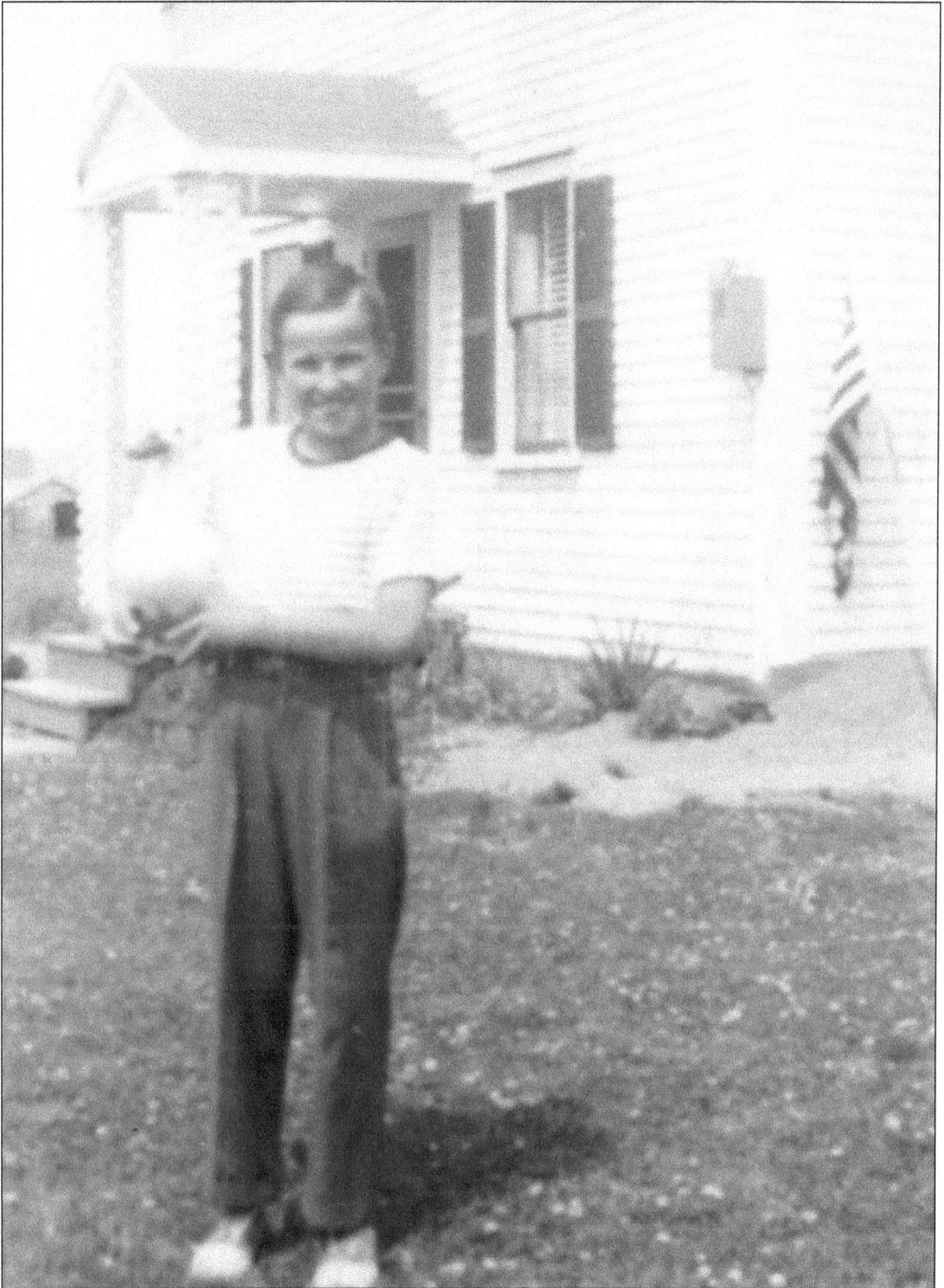

John L. Martin, 1949. This eight-year-old boy with a pet goose under his arm at Eagle Lake in the summer of 1949 became the speaker of the Maine House of Representatives and served for longer than anyone. John L. Martin now teaches political science and is in the admissions office at the University of Maine at Fort Kent. Born in Eagle Lake, he moved to Greenville for a few years (spending his summers at Eagle Lake) and then moved back to his native town, where he has lived ever since.

Emile Lucien Belanger (1894–1958) in 1948 at the age of 54. He was the owner of Baker's Machine Shop, Van Buren.

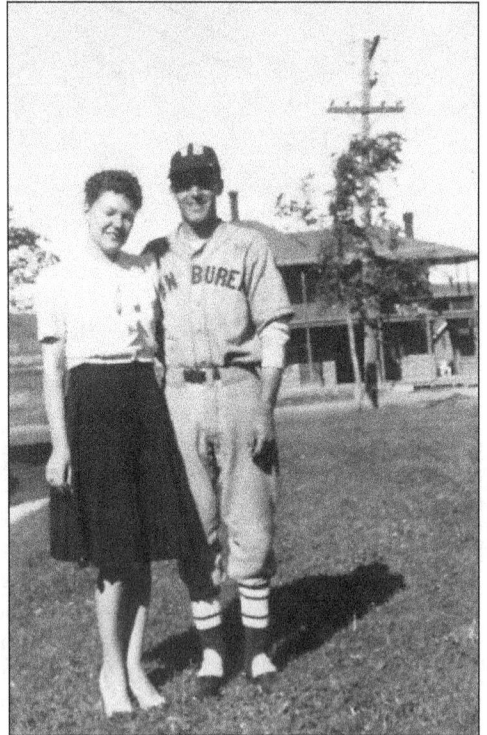

Elmer Violette and Marcella Belanger Violette in the summer of 1947 on Main Street, Van Buren. They had married in September 1946. The future Maine Supreme Court justice and Democratic Congressional candidate is in the uniform of the Van Buren Bulldogs in the Aroostook County League. He was a good-hitting (not for power) and good-fielding shortstop. The future justice was about to start in the Boston University Law School. His wife received a master's degree from B.U. and her Ph.D. from Laval University in Montreal.

The former residence of Major William Dickey in Fort Kent, c. 1950. The "Duke of Fort Kent" was one of the longest running Democratic state legislators in Maine history. Dickey was instrumental in founding the Madawaska Training School; he fought to have bridges placed over the St. John River; and he backed and won the land claims of Acadian settlers.

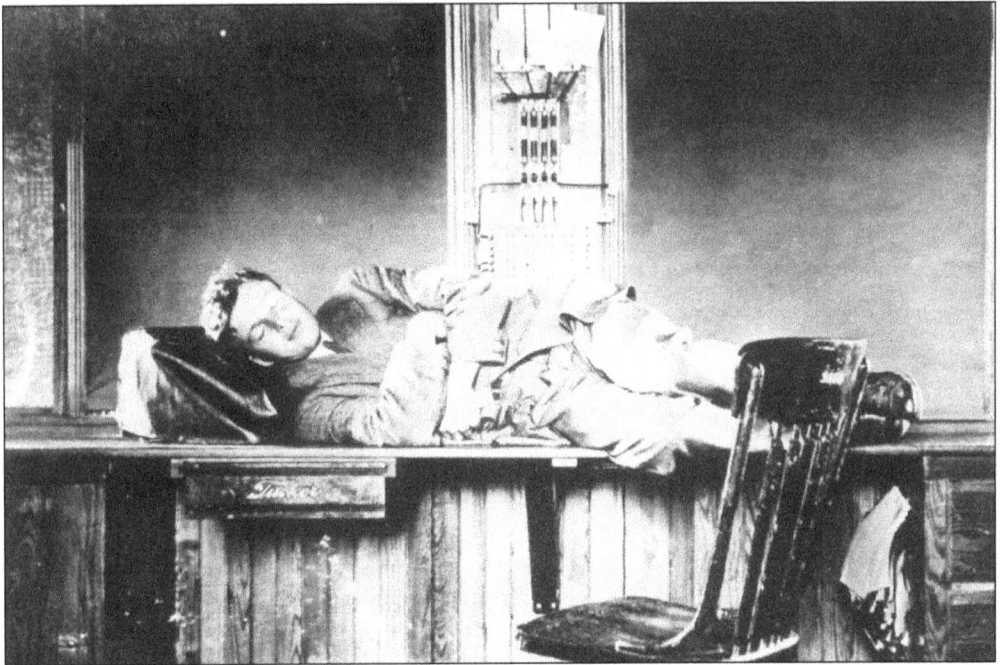

Madawaska train station. With the train already having left for Van Buren and paper shipments as yet a matter of the future, Elden Tapley, station agent in Madawaska, finds time for a wink or two. This was in 1911 or 1912 and illustrates the "sleepy" community Madawaska was before the arrival of the paper industry.

119

Alfred Dufour (son of Ubald Dufour and Lea Daigle) in his *c.* 1915 Studebaker. Alfred loved to travel.

Dr. Andrew N. McQuarrie (1911–1985) in the mid-1930s. Born in Sheridan, this osteopathic physician opened practice in Madawaska in 1938. In 1973, he was named Madawaska's outstanding citizen. For years, he examined Madawaska High athletes free of charge. He pushed for the fluoridation of water and formed the immunization program for area children. He was the Madawaska health director, served on the Madawaska School Board for 22 years, and loaned the town $5,000 to pay teachers when Madawaska had run out of money during the Depression. He was also chairman of the Madawaska Water District.

Madawaska Police Chief Fedime Morin and the Lions' Club Santa Claus (Lionel Poulin) in 1952.

Alsime Cyr, longtime barber in Madawaska, standing in front of his brother-in-law's hardware store next to Bouchard's clothing store, c. 1920.

John Vollman (1915–1975), founder of Northern Trading Co., in Madawaska. The company was famous as distributors of Jade East, which it sent through Swank Inc., and was known as a maker of body products for many of the country's largest distributors.

Rev. Lionel Thibodeau. While assistant pastor of St. Thomas Aquinas Parish in Madawaska from 1936 to 1943, he was instrumental in starting the campaign that resulted in the founding of the Madawaska Public Library.

Rev. D. Wilfrid Soucy. While pastor of St. Joseph's Church in Sinclair, Rev. Soucy was a great exponent of cooperatives during the Depression and was active in the founding of the St. John Valley Creamery cooperative. He also administered the mission to Guerette Plantation and was instrumental in having a road built from Sinclair to the Fort Kent-Caribou road.

Rev. Thomas Albert (1879–1924). Rev. Albert was the author of *L'Histoire du Madawaska*, published in 1920, in which he pulled no punches.

Louise Beaulieu, age ten, when she was confirmed on July 15, 1922, at St. David Church by Bishop Walsh of the Diocese of Portland.

Daimase Vaillancourt, the oldest resident of Eagle Lake in 1934, standing in the garden of St. Mary's Parish Rectory in Eagle Lake.

Damase and Christie (Gagnon) Vaillancourt of Eagle Lake in 1906. The couple was married in 1871 by a Canadian priest who traveled from church to church performing weddings and burials. This couple's fifth child, Israel Vaillancourt, was the first person baptized in St. Mary's Parish, the first church established in Eagle Lake.

Harold and Annie Dow in 1946. Harold was a Maine state game warden from 1917 to 1949. Here, the couple is sitting on logs they cut and peeled themselves. They built a camp on Nigger Brook, now Pelletier Brook.

William Mullen. William married Eliza Gallaher. His beard was red and he was said to be the only man in Allagash from "downstate." All the others came from Canada.

Florida Vaillancourt, postmistress at Eagle Lake more than 40 years, with her dog on the steps of her home at the age of 22, *c.* late 1930s.

Lewellyn Despres, age three, in 1938. He would grow up to teach at the University of Maine at Fort Kent. Despres has written a novel, *Cry, Michael, Cry,* and is working on another novel, which is almost completed.

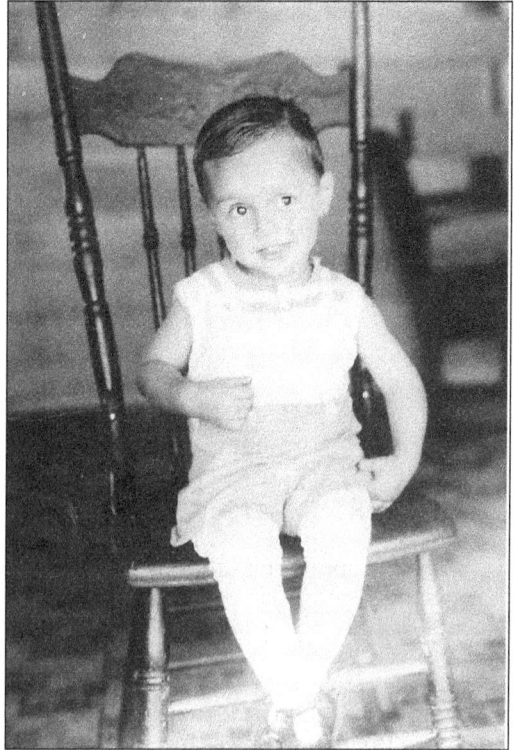

Remi Daigle of St. Agatha during World War I. He was a game warden and died in 1942.

Acknowledgments

Easily number one on this list is Mrs. Cecile Dufour Pozzuto of Madawaska. She has indexed the Madawaska Historical Society's collection of old photographs better than any other collection I have ever seen. She made herself available to me at every turn. Over 140 of the pictures in this book came though her. I first had to eliminate all photographs in the collection that were in her 1985 pictorial history of Madawaska. There were some 471 photographs left from which the final 140 plus were chosen. It made my 900-mile commutes from Portland all worthwhile. I would also like to thank Mrs. Pozzuto's sidekick, Norma Berube, for all her help.

Thanks go to Lisa Ornstein, director of the Acadian Archives at the University of Maine at Fort Kent for pointing me to Mrs. Pozzuto and others at the start of my investigation into the Valley. Former Maine Supreme Court Justice Elmer Violette and his wife, Marcella, directed me to the Archives and supplied many photographs. Former Speaker of the Maine House of Representatives John L. Martin told me about sources in Eagle Lake and supplied several images.

In Allagash, Faye O'Leary Hafford let me have some of her photographs. I was directed to her by Edith Kelly, president of the Allagash Historical Society. In Van Buren, John Pelletier, owner of Borderview Nursing Home, supplied pictures from the collection of his aunt, Martine Pelletier. Christie Cochran, who is the Washburn correspondent for the *Presque Isle Star Herald*, supplied photographs at a critical time in the book's production. In Eagle Lake, Lewellyn Despres provided a treasure trove of pictures. Florida Vaillancourt, Reynold Raymond, and Susan Soucie were also very helpful with providing interesting photographs. I cannot forget the many efforts of Patsy Theriault, head librarian in Madawaska.

This book would not have been possible if my cousins, Stan and Jackie Greaves of Presque Isle, had not been able to put up with me the many nights at their home, where I rested and got ready to go again. Without the help of their son, Tom Greaves, and their daughter and son-in-law, Ray and Sandy Gauvin, I would not have been able to survive my five-day stay in Presque Isle while waiting for a new radiator for my battered VW Fox. And John Jalbert, the head of Autotech in Presque Isle and a relative of famed Maine guide Sam Jalbert of Fort Kent, did everything he could and more to get me a new radiator.

Finally, I would like once again, in this—my tenth book for Arcadia—to thank the people at my publisher in Dover, New Hampshire. They are as follows: Jim Burkinshaw, the executive vice president; Rebecca Heflin, my editor; Becky Cooper; Jamie Carter; Michael Guillory; and Caroline Wolfe. I hope I can keep up the pace.

www.ingramcontent.com/pod-product-compliance
Lightning Source LLC
Chambersburg PA
CBHW080910100426
42812CB00007B/2229